Healing Beauty

Healing Beauty

Naomi M. Wong

RESOURCE *Publications* · Eugene, Oregon

HEALING BEAUTY

Resource Publications
An Imprint of Wipf and Stock Publishers
199 W. 8th Ave., Suite 3
Eugene, OR 97401

www.wipfandstock.com

PAPERBACK ISBN: 978-1-7252-9290-1
HARDCOVER ISBN: 978-1-7252-9291-8
EBOOK ISBN: 978-1-7252-9292-5

02/16/21

To all who have been a part of my healing journey

To my family and friends who have walked with me
in grace and mercy

To the beautiful God from whom, through whom,
and for whom is all beauty

Contents

Preface

Please consider this an appropriately placed trigger warning. *Healing Beauty* deals with topics that may dredge up unpleasant feelings or memories in the reader. I respect the reader's ability to decide how much to read at a time and whether to finish at all. I will give a small spoiler here to say that this book ends on a more positive note than the one on which it begins. Hopefully, this narrative can provide some proof that there is, indeed, true life beyond the events that we wish we could forget.

The structure of this book is meant to reflect the nonlinear experience of time that can accompany the effects of an emotional trigger. Each of the six sections begins with a poem related to a formative event or the thought pattern of a particular season in my healing journey. These events move in a sequence of meaningfulness rather than chronologically. In addition, the reader will notice that there are Bible verses from various translations placed before and after each section, verses that are sometimes used grossly out of context. This is purposeful. The oppression of vulnerable people has often been perpetuated through the use of out-of-context Bible verses as well as the picking and choosing of translations for the most convenient bolstering of one's own opinion. In this book, I attempt to mimic the odd contribution that this method of Scripture-use has made to my journey, for worse and for better. I leave it to the reader to decide the advantages and disadvantages of such a practice.

Introduction

The Black T-shirt and Jeans

There was a season of my life during which I always wore a black T-shirt and jeans to church. I did so out of sheer terror. A married member of my church's leadership was giving me unwanted attention, and I was desperately looking for a way to make it stop without causing a scene. I had already tried wearing baggy sweaters and sweatpants while neglecting to comb my hair. However, I eventually settled for the black T-shirt and jeans because the baggy clothes had not had the desired effect and good friends were beginning to ask about my strange behavior. I was afraid to tell them the truth, so I hoped that the black T-shirt and jeans would look normal enough to avoid suspicion. I also hoped that my new uniform would be casual and non-colorful enough to keep me from attracting unwanted attention.

As anyone might guess, the black T-shirt and jeans did very little to deter unwanted attention in that situation and, indeed, at the next church I attended. When these situations developed to a point at which confrontation became necessary, I learned that people in power often have very little incentive to admit to their own wrongdoing. These church leaders seemed to play a blame game, as if I had caused them to lust. One especially urged me to consider that the minds of men are simply different from the minds of women, that Christian women just do not understand how they can cause Christian men to stumble. It was perplexing to consider that I could somehow be blameworthy for situations in which I had been searching for every way not to be problematic.

The judgment remained. I therefore concluded that I was a vessel of destruction; that I was to blame for the wandering eyes and inappropriate behavior of adult people; and that I should not smile, look a person in the eye, say something funny, or wear dresses or anything colorful. "Beauty" was bad, untrustworthy, and blameworthy. I had a paralyzing fear of being seen because, if I were thought to be beautiful, *I* would be bad, untrustworthy, and blameworthy. These were the lies that I internalized, lies that poisoned my mind, constricted my life, and crushed my spirit.

At any moment, I could be blamed for a situation that I had never intended to cause and had even been consciously working against. The church, which had been my last safe place, began to merge with the world I already knew to be dangerous, lustful, and sometimes violent. And in this merging, the past overtook me and overwhelmed me. All of time seemed to happen at once, bombarding me with memories of events only my body had remembered, feelings of powerlessness, and a recognition of the desecration of the sacred image of God in me. Some may call these experiences "trauma." However, I have twice been told that my experiences are "not that bad," at least compared to some. I try not to make a habit of comparison since I have only my life to live, and I do not intend to blow my experience out of proportion or to minimize the experiences of others. That said, I have shared this bit of my background here in order to orient the reader to my position on the topics that I engage in my work. In this book, I write intentionally vaguely in the hopes that my particular experience will not distract the reader as we journey together.

A Drop in the Bucket

While not the first published, *Healing Beauty* is the very first book of poetry that I ever wrote. It is at the same time a creative portrayal of my experience, a confrontation of the double standards that many women face on a daily basis, inside of and outside of the church, and a testimony that the goodness of God transcends the misdeeds of people. As I came to terms with past and present wounding, I learned just how deeply all of my thoughts and relationships were afflicted by a faulty perception of beauty. The wrongness of beauty tormented me daily, but writing prayerfully provided one avenue of relief from this torment. The poems in this book, every one using a unique voice and structure, engage themes such as fear, survival, interpersonal relationship, relationship with self, body image, healing, and the redefinition of beauty.

It was through this writing process that I began to identify, confront, and purge the lies that I had internalized. I faced oppressive fears about people's poor responses to beauty, including my own. I wrestled with what it meant to exist in a world obsessed with ephemeral physical beauty. I also learned that true beauty is not based on anyone's opinion except that of the loving creator. The natural world pulses with beauty given to it by the one whose very being is love. And we, humans, are beautiful by virtue of the fact that we are unconditionally loved. Love is the beauty in which we live and move and have our being. This is the beauty that never erodes, never loses value, never fades. This is the beauty that hopes all things, believes all things, and endures all things. This is the beauty against which there is no law.

This book is about such beauty. However, the absolutely necessary process of purging internalized lies can be confusing, unrefined, and quite markedly ugly. I have included ugly, unrefined, and confused poems in *Healing Beauty* because I want to give an accurate representation of the healing journey. At any point, my words may rub the reader the wrong way. I hope that the reader will be able to maneuver around these rough areas so that his or her own journey may move forward as necessary. I also want to acknowledge that my voice is one of many and that my experience is one of many. As such, the sentiments and opinions expressed in this book are meant to be but a drop in the bucket. My desire is that, through witnessing this portion of my healing journey, the reader may be encouraged to continue to seek his or her own personal healing. The work of healing is not easy, but it is worth it.

Regardless of the extent to which our experiences differ, I urge all readers to consider what might need to change in our society and particularly in the church's view of beauty and of women. I include myself and other women in this exhortation because I know that we can internalize unhelpful views of femininity, beauty, and blame that divide us as much as they tear us down. Christians especially have a call to be transformed by the renewing of our minds,[1] both those of us who have been wronged as well as those of us who have been wrong. It is quite likely that many of us have been on both sides of the wronging across a variety of situations. I am not talking about blame anymore or about what people perceive to be blameworthy but about guilt before God. I am talking to those of us who abuse our power as well as to those of us abused by power who, in turn, tear down others. This has to stop, and the stopping starts with us. May we be transformed by the renewing of our minds.

A Note to the Church

Even though the anguish that pervades much of my poetry was not solely caused by my unfortunate experiences in the church, it would be remiss not to deal with some family business right now, especially in light of the #MeToo and #ChurchToo movements. The specific issues that I would like to highlight here are (1) the lack of commitment to self-control that leads to unchecked lust, especially in Christian men; (2) the blaming of women for the thoughts and actions of men; and (3) the gender-based double standards that lead women to mistreat each other. I firmly believe that Christians must encourage one another toward healthy patterns of thought and behavior. However, I have noticed that some Christian men seem not to take much responsibility for their own agency in this regard, particularly with respect to gender relations. This attitude and the behaviors that often accompany it contribute to a culture in which women are seen as responsible for the actions of men. Then, under this pressure, women turn against each

1. Romans 12:2 (NIV)

other and perpetuate the very same hurtful patterns that have been harming women for generations.

At least theoretically, Christians freely admit that we are all sinners in need of mercy, grace, and salvation. I would humbly submit that in addition to mercy, grace, and salvation given by Jesus Christ, we also need repentance, which we ourselves must enact. Repentance should involve a change of heart and a perceivable change in behavior. Individuals must be accountable for their own actions. Leaders, in particular, must not abuse their power through the belief that they may act with impunity. Communities need to support women, to believe women, and to respect women. I say this with great love and respect for the church and with a desire that we may all, both male and female, embody the character of Christ to each other and to the rest of the world. As I strive to do so, I also urge my sisters and brothers in Christ to "act justly and to love mercy and to walk humbly with" our God.[2]

So now, I invite the reader to join me on this path: to examine beauty, to seek to understand it, to see if it may be redeemed. The following section is a lamentation that I wrote at the height of my distress. I believe that it expresses well the brokenness of some popular views of beauty and the need for beauty to be healed.

The Problem with Beauty

Is it wrong to say that I'm tired of being "beautiful?" Tired of glassy eyes and dagger stares and mute men and indignant women. I'm tired of having multiple shadows; shadows with wives are the worst. I'm tired of hunting hands, hooting in the street, and the definition of wisdom meaning the acceptance of a life of fear. I'm tired of friendships based on a one-sided desire for sex and friendships in which murderous intention lurks beneath the tumultuous surface of one's feelings of inadequacy.

I'm tired of the public gaze that only sees the surface.

2. Micah 6:8 (NIV)

I know beauty is not something you just walk away from. I'm just tired.

But I want to write about beauty, not vanity's wild-goose chase nor the scoundrel's excuse. I want to write about beauty unpredictable by popular expectations and beauty not calculated by the sum of a woman's parts. I want to write about beauty that is both seen and known. I want to write about beauty recognized and understood and enriched by interaction. A beauty that does not have to be hidden away for safety or diluted to preserve another's pride. I want to write about beauty that shines forth as the sun in the day and as the moon or the whole host of stars at night, unapologetic in their resplendence.

I want to write about beauty, but I do not know how to see past its misuse and abuse, its twisted manipulation and descent into faded glory. I do not know how to disentangle beauty from blame or how to rebut the insult that beauty has become. I do not know how to dedefine the redefinition of beauty that replaced selflessness with lustful indulgence, or how to reestablish the value that beauty has lost. I simply do not know how.

But I want to write of beauty. Beauty that blossoms and fades as well as beauty that lasts forever. I want to write of beauty that changes and morphs and becomes ever more beautiful as well as beauty that could not change even if it tried. I want to write of beauty once broken now healed or of the beauty of passion and determination, the beauty of courage and nobility, of purpose and completion, the beauty that no one can steal or deface.

But I lack the vision for it.

I cannot write of beauty when it is trapped in the eye of the beholder.

How, then, can it be set free?

A gracious woman gets honor, and violent men get riches.

—PROVERBS 11:16 (ESV)

Ruination

The Confrontation

I see you
Towering in your influence
Above me
Cold sweat turns to clamminess
My heart is in my feet
And my fingers are nowhere
Yes, I know I have to
Do this
If not for myself
Then for the others
If there are others
Who will not stand up to you
For fear of disgrace
Or falling from your graces
I will do it for them, for us
For you, even, I will do it
Armed with my limp noodle
Duty, I follow after you
A cold, stiff, shambling corpse
Dead to you, dead to me
Dead to the pain
I know is coming

The Trigger Finger

Prey
Shredded, stringy skin
Self
Adaptable, fluid
Circling around and around
A finger,
Multiplying, branching
Reaching, chasing
Living,
Magnetic vise,
A lever,
Happens backwards
In its strongest form
Fear

Afraid
Of fingers groping in the dark
Exploring
Areas of restricted access
Where I'm hidden away
Magnetic fingers
Invade
Pull that trigger
And the trigger pulls me back in again
I'm a cart with no wheels
I'm a fish on a line
I'm a hawk on the wind
Ready to rise and dive

But the trigger, like a chain and hook,
Like a reel
It pulls me back in again

Rewind
Here it comes
You'll be a soldier and a fugitive
Whether freedom is a state of being
Or a state of mind
Better get running, sweetie,
And never look behind
Blind
Fleeing through this soft cement
Minefield
Tick tock, tick tock
Hard to know exactly when, but
One wrong step and it's you to blame
Then the trigger pulls me back in again

Weary
Beyond shredded
I'm threadbare and frayed
How much more was needed?
How much more than I gave?
Step out of self, shed that skin
And let her keep running
So the trigger won't pull her back in again
She's half-naked
She's all unraveled
Her string's stretched taut and thin
And that's when
BANG!
The trigger pulls me back in again

Survival

Animalistic
His desire
His sweat
His muscle
His will

Thus he taught me

Mitigation
By enticement
Appeasement
Backwards control
Enslavement of a people

We are people
Aren't we?
This is nothing new
And yet
It is a trap

I cannot
Not
Fall into
Because superficially,
At least

It works

I have him

Where

I want him

No, where

He wants me.

Modus Vivendi

Orgasmic impotence
Palliative invasion
Oppressive ecstasy

Penetration or fusion
Addiction or fear
Domination or entanglement

A consummation that breeds defeat
A moral chokehold

Deception

Intimate Jealousy

Judas-lips upon my cheek
Those poison, juicy, sucking lips
How she loves to hate me!
And how she hates to love me.

Derisive encourager in my face
Has those foul, scabby, lying lips
She's thirsty for my blood!
She'd give a pint to take one, too.

Hostile companion at my back
Has those loud, snarling, unspeaking lips
With one mouth, she caresses me,
With the other she twists her knife.

Bones and Blood

I grapple to contain this rapidly unraveling reality, my world possessed by the uncontrollable. I try to starve out the condemnation. And now, I realize I am only bones. Bones and skin with blood I can't get rid of. The skin is extra. I'm just bones. And blood.

The weight on the scale goes down. I disappear out of my clothes once, twice, three times. But I am as heavy as I ever was. I am irregular. I am cramping. I am bleeding lies. My fullness slips away, and I am an empty, stretch-marked bag. Well, empty but bulging with the blood, which I cannot get rid of no matter how hard I try, and the bones.

Now, I alone control everything that comes into my body, but I cannot control what comes out or if it will come out at all. I am fragile and split like the brittle glory that comes down from my head. My eyes are runny glass. Loose skin is like loose clothes draped on this awkward form, on my bones. The skin is extra. I'm just bones.

And blood.

No More Love

No more love!

No more strangulation mingled with kisses
No more sugarcoated death threats
No more cleverly phrased indoctrination

No more obsession and iron grips
No more strings wound round fingers
No more fear to yank me back in again

No more love!

It is oceans away
It is six feet under
It is on the other side

It is rock hard
It has decayed
It is only dust
Now.

No more love.

No more, love.

The Artist's Shoulders

I see the artist's shoulders at noon
Shoulders, bent but not broken
Under the weight of the world
And shredded, as we tend to be
Shoulders that take seriously the joke of skin
That's what I see, but
Skin as a preferred medium is a hoax
So, I turn my eyes away
Still, I cannot unsee them
The shoulders, like a womb or a shield
Striped
I am somewhere between
Woolly and wooden
But I feel an awful lot like spit
I hate that I came
From the mouth of a man
Putrid as his lies
Glistening, mocking, unwiped
On these shoulders
Resolute, intent
On using every medium
Even flimsy skin
To recreate the beauty they have borne
From the beginning

The glorious beauty is a fading flower which is at the head of the fertile valley, like a first-ripe fig before summer—whoever sees it, swallows it up while it is still in his palm.

—Isaiah 28:4 (TLV)

Rumination

They Say

Go jump in a lake of fire before we have to stone you
They say
Unacceptable, deplorable, dirty thing, you
They say
Any offering you bring is dirty like you
They say
Melt down, dissolve, take flight, or whatever you do
They say
Temptation to commit adultery smiles like you do
They say
Get out, stay out, bleed out like you do
They say
Sister-not-sister, we have it in for you
With love, we do.
They say

Life on the Margins

"Honey," she says, and pats his thigh
Her action is meant to be discreet
Intimate, gentle, commanding
She is calling him back from the edge
Where gallantry springs up
Alongside tares of goofy arousal

I am used to life on the margins
I am familiar with the thigh-pat
As familiar as I am with a woman's side-glance
The wrinkle of her nose and her plastic smile
She starts off trying not to blame me
There is no harm in an opinion, after all

Comparison

The scales of the beholder tip up and down
As fancy and passion toss weight on either side
And the mysterious connection of self-esteem adds
A heightened sensitivity .
So, we are pitted against each other
Isolated
Divided
Conquered

The Fault Lies with You

Never wear a short skirt
Because, really, any skirt is an invitation.
So, it's pants, then.
Not too tight, though, or else he'll see your curves.
But if they're too loose, he'll think that you are too.
And then, it would be your fault.

Never wear bright colors
Because colors are too eye-catching.
So, wear only the drabbest of hues. No prints.
Such clothing becomes a gentle, quiet spirit.
But be aware he may find that attractive.
And then, it would be your fault.

Never smile at him
Because guys find smiles flirtatious.
So, those are out.
But if you don't smile at all,
He'll think you're playing hard to get.
And then, it would be your fault.

Never look a man in the eyes
Because that's the language of allurement.
So, always evade his gaze.
But when you do, take care.
He might strive for your attention.
And then, it would be your fault.

Miss Thing

Miss Thing,
Fancy little skin you're in
You pretty little trinket lady
All manmade material
Painted, dainty so
Turn you over and over
Stick something in
Squeeze something out
And set you on a shelf
For all to see
Lovely girl, you
Stay right there
And never change

The Friendzoner

We're a disaster in the making,
A ticking time bomb that makes
An act of kindness turn abomination
An act of hatred just another day

Dx: Terminal Desire

Early onset. No known cure. Aggressive treatments would be a catalyst for decline.

For a while I pretend not to notice that you sneak a compliment or declaration of love very unsubtly into unrelated conversation. But the closer you assume yourself to be, the further away you slip. You believe that success is a matter of swiftness, pure brawn, and cunning. But all I ask for is the space to breathe. Any animal can pursue, corner, and maul. I've seen it time and again.

A word of warning: you may tear my flesh to shreds and never ever find me.

I abhor the sparkle in your eye. My scent in your nostrils. What shallow breath you breathe. Unbearable. The loss I feel when you begin to turn our conversation toward the act that you desire. It always goes back to that one thing.

Can my personhood be reduced to a sensory experience?

Our friendship is in slow decline. You will first experience light-headedness, then a pain in your chest. Increased aggression and mood swings are common. As we near the end, you will give me an ultimatum. And then, maybe for my safety or for your pride, the end will come.

The Inmate's Lament

It's no house of bricks
Or *Dame de Fer*
It's just a prison
That's all.

I'm inside here still
But you'd rather talk to a wall
An unstable, deteriorating prison
Wall.

Insecurities

A day will come when time prevails

When what's smooth is rough
And what's shiny is dim
When what's abundant and glossy
Is barren and dull
When what's perky sags
And the curves are more like rolls

A day will come when all news is old news

When the catching and subduing have been done
And the chase is no longer on
When all that was valued has been enjoyed
And the fun is over
When these prison walls erode
And all that's left is me

Consolation

I have only ever been pleasing
To your sight
Just a shallow film of sweetness
Over pain
Your so-called "love" is non-perishable
In practice, at least
If it's just a lifeless image you want
That's how I'll never change
This smile will be yours, always
This flesh warm to your imagination
This heart eternally isolated
That is the depth of your love, and
It is my only consolation to know that
There is but one gate that leads to life
And it is not you

Will Power

I will not be your last temptation
So, stop looking at me like
Conquering me will save your world

Be reminded: I never asked for your attention

If you brag about your
Commitment to another woman
Then, you should walk the walk

And take a walk while you're at it

Following me to prove you can
Resist your desires
Is indicative of a weak will

And possibly the end of the world

Love as Forsaken

Let's get one thing straight: I'm no home-wrecker
But home-wreckers often search me out
And the sincerity of their infatuation has taught me
Love as forsaken

This is what has become of love
That I've learned to rejoice when
Men can no longer bear to look at me
To applaud when they flee from my presence

To celebrate their dismissal of my opinions
When everything that reminds them of me is
Taken out with yesterday's trash
Because, finally, they have turned

From cheap and meaningless desire
To love the woman they have committed to
"Forsaking all others"
I am all other

This is how I learned love as absence

Love as dismissal
Love as redirection and rejection
Love as undesire
Love as forsaken

My Brother's Keeper

With one golden ring missing
You are fading to monochrome
And since you keep buzzing around
I am reminded that I am my brother's keeper

Separation comes as a relief to you because
Your queenright status became a bitter thing
But so would the sweetness of fresh honey
That drips from virgin combs

No one will measure up, humanly speaking
Momentary passion would be found wanting
In the presence of childlike sincerity
Your need to be loved

A bitter veil hides this vain compassion
Toward multifaceted eyes that only see desire
And yet the goodness of pre-established sanctity
Bolsters the fortitude of this boundary

Make a beeline, sir, back to your hive.

Like a gold ring in a pig's snout is a beautiful woman
who shows no discretion.

—PROVERBS 11:22 (NIV)

Reaction

Suck It Up!

"Suck it up!" I told her, "for the ones you love.
"I mean, do you know what this kind of news will do to them?"

"You're right," she said, and sucked it up.

So, she carried our secret until her back was twisted and bent.
She came to me and said, "We're falling apart from the inside out.
"I'm rotting, and people are starting to ask about the smell."

"Suck it up," I told her. "Think about what they'll do to us.
"You have no proof, and I'll be ridiculed to death!"

So, she protected the secret to save me from blame
But deteriorated until only the secret remained

When the secret came back with a bat,
I looked away in shame
It smashed my frame to smithereens
Then, the secret stared into the glass
And chuckled, "Suck it up!"

Hands

There are some who have hands for eyes
And hands for ears and noses, too
They have hands for tongues
But they have tongues for hands
And they indulge their tastes far too often

Confronting Hedges

Sir, do you think me ill-humored if I do not smile at your crude statements? Or do you think me proud to notice at all that you are an orbiting, lidless eyeball? Is it unladylike to call out and rebuke your boorish, caveman-like advances? I'd ask you to excuse my indignation at the assumption that I must ask you to respect me, but I can't.

Hi. Still listening? I'd like to turn inside out and punch you in the face, but perhaps you'd think me too pure of heart. Ah! Still listening. Just checking. Inner beauty might still be conducive to anger at injustice, if you don't mind my saying.

But if I am to use civil words to combat your uncouth behavior, then I just hope you will excuse my not asking your forgiveness in saying:

Let me tell you where you can shove that double standard . . .

The Eyes of the Beholder

Beholders' eyes are ugly
There is no beauty in them
That they might truly see

Their eyes are filled with images
Of a goddess or a steak or trash
Where a person ought to be

Beauty was, until their lids
Unfolded and revealed
Their thoughts about me

Beholders' eyes are ugly
There is no beauty in them
That they might truly see

The Love of Cruelty

Backhanded compliments are child's play
It takes well-honed skills and finesse
To pull off a long-term autoimmune attack
Since we're all members of the same body

Love, family, *koinonia*, and all that

Oh, don't be so defensive; trust
Share, share, and be laid bare
Humiliation is our game
And we win

Lessons

Scars are lessons learned
I've been the new girl on the block before
I've been the talk of the town
I've been the social piñata
While I played the clown

Like a bludgeon
Is the multitude of saccharine words
That cheapen friendship
And now,
I know that closeness is more than skin on skin

Like a corrosive
Is the slow-burning glimmer of hatred
Entrenched in half-admiring eyes
And now,
I can discern the undertone of derision in praise

Like a cat-o'-nine-tails
Is the stubborn belief that a jealous person
May have a crisis of conscience
And now,
I know to look over my shoulder often

Love me like you do
I cannot withhold my love
From you,
Though I've learned to withhold
Myself

I Am the Potter

My hands are dirty
Ashes and tears mix into mud
They will harden into clay, but

If I am soft and moldable
It is not for you, or him, or anyone
If there is any form taking shape
It is not what I have yielded to

It is what I have chosen to become
To finish the formation I have begun
My hands are dirty

Functional Safety

I told it to be cold as I
Spoke it from clay into alabaster
It keeps the goods safe
With no color that might attract
Unwanted attention

I made it hard
Very, very hard
It keeps the fragrance away
From sensitive noses
With an airtight lid

The Only One

I am a wolf's howl on a crisp, fall evening
I am the island furthest from every shore
I am an oasis in the desert

I am the singular hump of a wandering dromedary
I am second in line, moonless, and hot
I am a goldfish in a bowl for all to see

I am the final ember amidst a pile of soft gray ashes
I am the avocado at the top of the tree
I am the oyster's long-awaited pearl

I am the southernmost *aurora borealis*
I am Halley's Comet come to visit
I am the sundog in which false messiahs see destiny

I am the only one.

Dissociation

Where have I withdrawn to?
And when will I be back again?
How can I end this endless retreat?
I know I'll stand, but I don't know when

I bob beneath the stormy surface
And fight for breath, between flows and ebbs
No sooner have I come into self, the pain
Plunges me back down to the depths

The waves, they just keep coming
I'm awash and alone in dread
Torture is the shore in front
And a wall of water overhead

I cannot keep up the struggle
This fight to get to shore
Then, when least-expecting toes reach out
Their groping skims the sandy floor

Admission

There is a whole lot of ugly in the world
And I look in the mirror for answers
But the beauty found there is of little
Assistance
Silence is too loud
But hearing the pain is worse
Or the same
I spend so much time running from it
From the pain, I mean
But then my life wanes
In the waxing of
Avoidance
It takes up so much space
But it is easier than
Admitting
I
  am
    broken

The Survivor's Question

The answer is not within me. I've looked within. Oh, I've conjured up all kinds of alter egos and self-preserving, positivity-dependent, pain-avoiding defense mechanisms. I've tried that inner light thing and found the strength in myself. It left me weak, empty, bitter, and rageful. I've not cared and moved on more than the average person. I've let go and let go and let go, but the pain of the past, the condemnation and shame, this feeling of dirt I cannot wash off, it all keeps coming back.

I must not be trying hard enough because anything should be possible for the determined woman.

No one can accuse me of a lack of commitment. I've drunk the poison of relational suicide for the sake of love, and I've cut off rotting limbs to be able to keep moving. I've died and died to keep surviving. And I have not survived this long without resolve. I've compartmentalized all the inefficient emotions. I've recreated myself and decided that pain doesn't hurt. I've become a thousand things to a million people and pulled myself out of the mire only to realize I was diving instead of climbing. I've been dashed to pieces and ground to powder. Countless times I have risen from the ashes to flourish and then to burn again until even the ashes have been scattered to oblivion.

So, where is the answer?

Because it doesn't originate from these messes that I call "me."

Cobweb in the Love Corner

Midnight moonlight on the cobweb
In the love corner illumined
Freshly woven fly trap (not Venus's)
Connects the walls with
Supple, silver, silken lines
Draped in a shape they flatter and
Aglow with the brilliance of the moon

In the love corner, too soon
Descends time's decay
Angry shadows on all things former
Reveal reality regarding the precious
Wispy cobweb in the corner
Fragile, holey cobweb love
Here today and gone forever

Lamented long, but started never
Tiny triangle between the walls
With such unreliable skin
Veiling only emptiness within
Love corner
Brought to nothing by dead flies
And jokesters with sticks

Starry-Eyed Dreamer

Starry-eyed dreamer
With the Milky Way smeared across your face
Live and love a night away
Fantasizing about men of flesh
Who see a soul beyond your sparkling ashes

Now you will understand

As morning dew
And snow in spring
Go up in vapor

So laughter dies and camaraderie turns to smoke
Temporary significance arbitrarily ascribed
And necessarily derived from a greater love than
This

He has made everything beautiful in its time. Also He has put eternity in their hearts, except that no one can find out the work that God does from beginning to end.

—ECCLESIASTES 3:11 (NKJV)

Recollection

Redemptive Love

Redemptive love, come find me
And make evident the over-ogled and under-seen
Draw me out of the comfortable dark places
Where I've hidden in morbid security
Walk with me through the rawness of vulnerability
And teach me how to bear the gaze of others
Redemptive love, relentless love,
Whose regard, while piercing, does not assail me,
Redemptive love, beautiful love,
Replenish me with blessed reassurance
Find me and invite me

Redemptive love, kind and gentle
Speak into my abandonment
Heal me with your constant presence
Flow down into all the cracks and roughest places
Wash away the pain and grime
That I may see again
That, with love, I may be full again
Love to trickle, then to flow
Around and through and deeper
Yes, deeper
Redemptive love, precious love,
Relentless, beautiful love
Come find me
See me, know me, and heal me

Amen

A Stone for a Rose

How loud a silence
Does a tiny stone create
When tossed into freshly fallen snows?
Visual capture gives way to disappointment
And all that remains are the resounding echoes
Of unfulfilled anticipation
Change would have been audible resonance
In that lifeless lack of auditory sensation
So in not hearing, I must see
And in seeing must the witness be
Of a red, red rose that grows
From those freshly fallen snows

Now in the silence reverberate
The themes determined to evade avoidance
Of course, they come at a cost
And as the shames recur,
I am reminded of prices paid for love lost
And truth valiantly searched after
Of happier days, now a haze
Of tears drowned out by laughter
I walk heel-first into the future
While the past unfolds before me
But the red, red rose, as everyone knows,
Professes or declares or invites without imploring

Also a fact well known:
A hemorrhage in the stone begins
When it understands loneliness,
Not the feeling, but the state
So living demands some openness,
A choice I know not how to make
Only fools would exchange a stone
For a red, red rose
That had out of frosty powder grown
But only embittered souls would dig in
Freshly fallen snows
For the stone that had been hidden

My Wounds, My Trophies

My wounds, my trophies
My pain, my strength
My oppression, my protection

My longing, my hangup
My heart, my weakness
My healing, my fairytale

The evil, the beauty
The confrontation, the nonsense
The deception, the truth

The Beauty and Beast

Is she still lovely with those claw marks across her face?
Be grateful because she's the one who keeps me from
Lopping off the hands of handsy men
And stringing them up as a warning
I bet if I did, though, she would not be thought of as so
Intoxicatingly demure
Regardless, she's bargained on our behalf
And I guess that's why we're still here today

So, we're stuck
I within
And she without
I seethe and she smiles
And we wonder if our aim is the same
Thinking maybe only our methods differ
But as the red, red rose begins to fade
I am becoming aware that we must
Learn to love each other
Before the last petal falls

Matter over Mind

I must not fall back on rage to be my strength
I must not entice to save my skin
I must not make evasion a habit
I have resolved to be different
And yet, when he comes at me
I struggle with matter over mind
Bombarded with flashes of failure,
All I see are my arms like toothpicks
Next to his
And his shadow engulfing mine
All I hear are my feet on the pavement
My heart beating for a few more seconds
And when I can think again, I wonder
How I will ever convince myself
Truly
That survival is no way to live

The New Cellmate

There's a new girl in here
I've stopped talking to her because I think she's scared of me
She cries whenever I look at her
But when I look away, I know she's watching me
And when I sleep, she creeps over
I feel her embracing me as she whispers, "Who am I?"

Something Worth Loving

Time is running out
And the closer I get to overlooked,
I panic,
Pouring all I've got into this jar
And praying
That when the prison is in a shambles
Something will remain,
Something worth loving.

What We Cannot See

Because we yearn for what we cannot see
We are spurred on by insatiable desire
In this time-long struggle for control

If we could paint love on our faces, we would try it
Just as we dream to slap a price tag on beauty
To make it attainable
We settle for the calculables
Of waist-to-hip ratio or, at best, give-and-take

But if we did not attempt to possess or control beauty
If we invited beauty on beauty's own terms
Could we not stumble upon the fulfillment of our longing?

Pain Is Gain

When love was false
I was nourished by sugar-encrusted air
The warmth of absolute zero
Tingling in my special places
Throngs of discordant ballads
Serenaded me like night terrors
Whispering reminders of love
I now hate

I hate it that
I long for the days when
With flushed face and simper
I thrived on empty praise and banter
From the sincerest of mouths
I long for the days when
With laughter and festivals
I jubilantly mourned for love
Whose absence I would not foretell
I long for the days when
With rotting gold
I bought an innutritious banquet
For every meal

How I gorged myself on the trifles of flesh
And wasted away clinging to its warmth
For comfort's sake!

Now in the simplicity of death,

The prospect of life seems daunting

Sacrifice sticking to my ribs

I am starved of pleasure to know

True intimacy

Love is pain.

Immanuel

My blood, your blood, our blood
Stains this empty room,
This "already."
Facing the opposite sky
Deformed by ridicule and shame,
Naked and shafted
It's me. And it's you.

So, I release my screams silently
Knowing that they'll reach the ears of
One.

Your hands stretched wide
Unable to wipe the tears
Bleeding
From your eyes into mine
Breathing rain
The reconciliation of my gaze
To the love that always saw me

A love in darkness felt
And in our ears ringing
A hope that suffers,
Screaming,
"Why have you forsaken me?"
With me.
With me.
With me.

Who do you think you are, and what are you doing here, building a beautiful tomb for yourself—a monument high up in the rock?

—Isaiah 22:16 (NLT)

Regeneration

Intercession of the Hunter's Daughter

So, there I knelt upon the altar, named
The hunter's latest sacrifice, ashamed
But through the tears, a sweetness in my ear,
A whisper of a child's voice I hear
"Sister, sister, do not be afraid
Sister, fearfully and wonderfully made."
How could I tell her of the hunter's chase,
How unrelenting and unchaste?
And how from fatigue my legs had failed me
In his inner wound where he impaled me?
"My sister, why, you have your mother's eyes!"
I knew to love our father was unwise
After double weight for twice my life, I cried
And the hunter's daughter held me as I died.

All I ever wanted was to make him proud
And I became to him a secret in a shroud
Bearing his false doctrine and his guilt
Within my womb was this stronghold built
But the hunter's daughter spoke to me of greatness
While I lay entombed in vagueness
Where can one hide from the eyes of a child
To keep her sweet gaze undefiled?
Yet through my terror and my shame
Not knowing that she knew my name
She reached into my grave to show me honor
Then, for just one moment, did I see our truest father
Who offers, through a child, our lasting peace
Legitimate for illegitimate, for our release

Love-Presence

If you are with me, then we are lonely together
In the mingling of our tears
And the sharing of our breath
Perhaps you have begun a work in me
If I know that my pain cannot be hidden from you
And that you will not turn your face away
Or grimace at the rawness of my flesh

Then our intimacy begins gently
Like the linking of pinky fingers
Or the gift of a wilted clover blossom
At the bottom of a playground slide
And we are braided throughout the years
Retroactively yet thoroughly woven into
Ever-renewing love,
Love that stays

Love at True Sight

Knowing love at first sight is to know the spite of an adoring glance,
The foreshadowing of a lonely future, every time it happens
That look being the negation of friendship
Just a passion, a steam-fogged mirror
In which the viewer only sees the self
Some intense minutes later
It is a romance, a ruiner of relationships,
A poor but common foundation shaken by
The seismic event called "disappointment" or just "reality."

But to be seen is a wondrous thing
It is to know the touch of the eyes as well as of the heart,
A delving-in that is less invasive than surface observation
It is a gentler discovery and tender understanding,
A calm focus and undemanding attention
That, on a heart which has been mauled
By the harshness of too many suitors
Unwilling to accept the fact of unrequited feelings,
Is a soothing balm and the truest healing salve.

Secret Perfume

I live in awe
Of this artist,
This miracle worker, this
Revolutionary lover
It sounds wrong when *I* say it
Someone with my past, someone
Chased away and exiled by ridicule

But in the secret of my prison,
I have mustered the entirety of my praise
The glorious mess of colors and light
Given in to weakness, I let it flow
Into this jar,
Oil of a sweet aroma
That only the creator knows

Your Gaze

You have locked on my heart
But there is no command in your mouth
I do not know how to be
With you

Your love does not devour me
It does not suck or slime
It does not invade or penetrate
In short, your love respects me

But your respect feels distant
Compared to the intimacy
Of personal and tyrannical
Oppression

The Spectrum

The canvas besmeared with pink and orange and sparkles
Here and there
The turquoise peaks and valleys or their white echoes
And swirling sprays
A sprawling green carpet seen from a high up place
Blurry, soft, and lush

An innocent one that slumbers in tranquil majesty
And stops the world with a yawn and cooing
The carefree laughter that ends in snorts
And the smiles shared thereafter
A kind word at just the right time
Or silence when no words suffice

The voice that stops deception in its tracks
And the heart that holds justice and mercy as complements
The hope of an embrace after a long separation
And the stirring of empathy in a thawing heart
The delicate skin beneath a peeling scab
And the realization that the world keeps on turning

The knowledge that what *is* is not all there is
And to look forward to what will be

One day

My Scars, My Monuments

My scars, my monuments
My chains, my enemy
My endurance, my celebration

My goal, my consecration
My spirit, my distinction
My desire, my calling

The perverse, the disease
The fight, the necessity
The truth, the freedom

Now I Know

That there is beauty that looks like beauty
That beauty can be found in transformation
And that all mortal beauty is borrowed
Whether we are born with it
Or we wash it off at the end of the day

True beauty has come upon me
Illuminating every dark place
In splendor and glory
I have nowhere to hide
And yet, I am unafraid

Prison, I Do Not Hate You

Prison, I do not hate you
I am sorry that I defaced your walls
And inner rooms
I trashed your courts and gardens
Your interrogation rooms and holding cells
Are a wreck because of me

I know you have only done your job
From the beginning, you did your best
You were assigned to me
And how ungrateful I have been
Only now I realize it since you are eroding
Because I pushed you too hard, I know

I did not feel that I could defend you
And so I often abandoned you
Sometimes, I used you as a distraction
So I could save myself
Prison, you deserved better
Better than me

Perhaps someone else would have
Maintained you well, painted your walls
Called you a sacred space and filled you
With decorations and treasures
Called you a home, temple, or fortress
Though a temporary one, you are

Is it too late?

What Is Living

Darkness blown to oblivion
Wind comes rushing through this temple, a blast
My throat ignites because of the unseen around me

Skin crumpling away like rotten cloth
Luminescence is my being seen, at last
Sparkles annihilate the veil that bound me

From night to light
From earth to sky and space
See now, what is living
Light

Together Again

Curiously unalarming
Fiber on fiber is flesh over bone
Substantial coverage
And blood coursing through it
The way it really ought to
Yes, even skin can hold it in
For its short time and small space
Nearness is success

Unsettlingly delightful
Wobbling pieces work together
Hesitant unison
And blood restoring feeling to it all
The way it really ought to
Yes, even to the heart that pumps
For new experience and new memories
Together again

Another Day One

How little makes sense to me now
Only that I apparently still am
The fullness of a great destiny
Lost on me
In this sensory overload
Repeat performance
Or existence
For those who missed the first
Day One

To the Leader of an Army

What do you see?
Piercing through death
Onto a valley of bones
Dry and shriveled
Blind, mouthless
Silent
I hear
A voice
Calling out
To the wind from Earth's four corners
Entering the mocking arena
To heal and raise up
"Talitha kum!"
Stand and eat
And you will live again
Then, speak

A Daring First Breath

Pain cannot be the only art
Nor anger the only strength
Nor brokenness the only beauty

The state of the world has revealed what I am
However

I have a calling higher than to what is
A calling to what can and must be
Not to transcend my humanity
But for it to be fulfilled
Through my becoming the recipient agent
Not a pawn or patient, but a partner
For healing, for wholeness, for peace

Though once despised and hated and rebuffed by all, you will be beautiful forever, a joy for all the generations of the world, for I will make you so.

—ISAIAH 60:15 (TLB)

Reconsecration

Alabaster Heart

Compassionate cords everlasting
Drawing me closer
Love, in kindest earnest, calling
Wordlessly through the fog
Of wrinkled noses and condescending gazes
Fear and shame clinging to my
Body
And I am clinging to this colorless, stone
Vessel
I tip the jar, but pull it
Back
This was a mistake.
I thought I could brave the ridicule
And blame,
But—
Still, this love is
Calling me, drawing me
I approach you from behind
Thinking
You may not
notice
me
Reaching, intending
From desperate premeditation to
Touch you
Yes, to adore you
With tears from dirty, lustful eyes
To wash your feet

And with scented, seductive hair
To dry them
And with unclean lips to kiss you
Just imagine what they will think of me
Unacceptable, yes.
  Inappropriate, wasteful adoration stemming
   From unwarranted, costly, precious mercy
   Irrevocable
    This alabaster heart now kneeling
    Responding
     Yes

Not the Only One

I am not the only one
To walk away feeling dirty
To wish I had reacted faster
To shoulder blame for being "flirty"

To cry alone in the bathroom
I am not the only one
To have my hands on my mouth
To keep my pain from everyone

To shout at the mirror:
Why don't you see me for real?
I am not the only one
To respond: No one *cares* how you feel!

To decide I'll wait for them to throttle me
To decide after that to run
To decide I'll fight instead of flee
I am not the only one

Do Not Pity Me

Sister, do not pity me
Cry with me; let's commiserate
Maybe share our scars to celebrate
But please, my sister, do not pity me

I'm a victim no longer
Undefined by words of blame
Never to be the same
I'm a survivor, stronger

No, sister, do not pity me.

We can see each other well
In the common spaces of our wounds
Perhaps we can change our tunes
In order to cooperate and excel

We will face the centuries
With courage through the pain
Sister, together we are sane
And we will make new memories

So, let's do away with pity.

Sister, we are overcomers
We are weathered and tried
We've shriveled and died
But now, we are the forerunners

We must not cling to pity
Our tears are dry of tears
Finally, we have faced our fears
And so have no need for pity

Even This

Your work has been proven
Hay, wood, and stubble
Though rejected, I am your gold
Your prizes have become ash
And I am gold because
You killed me. Weep
If it leads you to repentance
Turn from your ways!
When you crushed me
Pain became my co-suffering
And death my healing
Rising to new life, I see you
Remaining in the death you chose
It is because I am glorified with love
That we call you with one voice:
Come forth!

Outpouring

I am
Stardust, love dust
All natural and supernatural materials

Yearning to exchange human-made trinkets
For a life which is a result of
The greatest creative love-outpouring

Incomparable
Even sunlight becomes like shadows
In the brilliance of this love

Can I hide the greenery of the land
Or the waves of the sea?
As much as I can hide a wildfire under a basket!

I am loved
And so I am
All the natural world sings with me

For, now, flowers burst from my skin
And streams of water flow from my heart
I am alive and free to live

It Pulls Me Back

BANG!
Loose lips sank ships
Now my skin's unzipping
And I'm exposed
Infidel
Heaving and retching
Hiding, if I can
He finally found a way in
The pestilence which stalks in darkness
Temptress
Voices in my skin
Bats and bugs all over me
Hot breath and hair in my face
I awake in the fetal position
This again
My arms fall away from my head
I swing my legs over the side of the bed
I'm back, but at least, this time,
I am in the land of the living

Beyond the Walls

This is not where my story ends
Not between two constricting walls
Not with this double vision
Of abandonment overlaid with purpose

Sleeping through the night is an attainable sweetness
Possible most nights, though not a given
And courage to walk through a group of men
Still a goal

But I know there's something beyond these walls

On one side, I'll have peace to stand wherever
And to wear sweatpants, if I please
Even if there is room for a body
Behind me

On the other side, I will need no rage
To give me courage for the fight
And enticement, my second nature,
Will waste away from disuse

Today, Healing Looks Like

Today, healing looks like taking three steps instead of two
And shedding two tears instead of three
Since my eyes are that much drier
Maybe I can hope for the day I'll run a mile
But today,
I'll lift my head that much higher
And pray for strength to lift my other foot
So that, tomorrow, it might come down again

Sweet Fragrance

Love is the joy set before me
Which transforms sweat like blood
Into droplets of hope
Making my head sacred
And every rejection by our own
A greater reception in rebirth
Empowerment to this precious
Anointing

Powerfully Beautiful

Powerfully beautiful
Desirous hope
Instilled by a loving heart
Despite my wandering, a gift
Forgiven eyes now opened to
A new end, a good start
A vision of unapologetic existence

Powerfully beautiful
Shallowly delectable
Now not-so-suggestible
Profoundly transformed
With a mind reformed

Solid

Firmly anchored in
A kind and constant
Love-presence,

Beauty.
To walk among the people
Not for their appraisal
But to *be*
With due acknowledgement
To the master artist,
I will be

A glorious masterpiece
Not to entrust my heart to all
(For I know the human heart)
But to break this alabaster jar,
And then, in simple joyous freedom
To live, and speak, and dance
And burst into colors, if I want to

All reflecting the compassionate beauty
That was and is and is yet to come
Calling me

I will be

Yes, a woman
Who may be noticed,
But not known at a glance

Yes, I will be

Powerfully beautiful,
Endowed by love.

. . . and the house was filled with the fragrance of the perfume.

—John 12:3b (NASB)

CPSIA information can be obtained
at www.ICGtesting.com
Printed in the USA
FSHW020302270321
79762FS